B
X

WITHDRAWN

Malcolm X

JUNIOR ■ WORLD ■ BIOGRAPHIES

A JUNIOR *BLACK AMERICANS OF ACHIEVEMENT* BOOK

Malcolm X

DAVID SHIRLEY

CHELSEA JUNIORS

a division of CHELSEA HOUSE PUBLISHERS

FRONTISPIECE: *The 1960s' most controversial and charismatic leader, Malcolm X, was at his best before a crowd.*

Chelsea House Publishers

EDITORIAL DIRECTOR Richard Rennert
EXECUTIVE MANAGING EDITOR Karyn Gullen Browne
EXECUTIVE EDITOR Sean Dolan
COPY CHIEF Robin James
PICTURE EDITOR Adrian G. Allen
ART DIRECTOR Robert Mitchell
MANUFACTURING DIRECTOR Gerald Levine
PRODUCTION COORDINATOR Marie Claire Cebrián-Ume

JUNIOR WORLD BIOGRAPHIES

SENIOR EDITOR Ann-Jeanette Campbell
SERIES DESIGNER Marjorie Zaum

Staff for MALCOLM X
EDITORIAL ASSISTANT Kelsey Goss
PICTURE RESEARCHER Sandy Jones
DESIGNER John Infantino
COVER ILLUSTRATION Alan Nahigian

3 5 7 9 8 6 4

Library of Congress Cataloging-in-Publication Data
Shirley, David.
    Malcolm X / David Shirley.
        p. cm.—(Junior world biographies)
    Includes bibliographical references and index.
ISBN 0-7910-2106-8
        0-7910-2112-2 (pbk.)
    1. X, Malcolm, 1925–1965—Juvenile literature. 2. Black Muslims—Biography. 3. Afro-Americans—Biography. I. Title. II. Series.
BP223.Z8L5773 1994   93-17700
320.54'092—dc20   CIP
[B]   AC

Contents

1   Back in New York   7

2   Malcolm Little   17

3   Detroit Red   31

4   Malcolm X   45

5   The Final Days   63

     Further Reading   73

     Glossary   74

     Chronology   76

     Index   78

An outspoken advocate for racial justice, Muslim minister Malcolm X inspired his followers and disturbed countless other listeners with an angry, relentless assault on the crimes and abuses of white society.

1

Back in
New York

It was a sunny May afternoon at Kennedy International Airport, and the mostly white New York City press was buzzing with excitement. Malcolm X, the city's most controversial black leader, was scheduled to arrive on the next flight from Cairo, Egypt. More than 50 local reporters and photographers were crowded into the waiting room. Each hoped to hear the first words spoken by the fiery *Muslim* minister as he emerged from the customs gate.

When Malcolm X had left for Africa the month before, there had not been a crowd of reporters to see him off. Only his family and closest friends were at the airport to wave good-bye as he boarded the jetliner that would take him first to Frankfurt, Germany, and then on to Cairo. Malcolm's final destination, however, was *Mecca,* the Holy City of the religion of *Islam* and birthplace of the prophet Muhammad. To get there, he would have to travel another 2,000 miles south from Cairo, across the Red Sea into Saudi Arabia.

Each year more than 1 million devout Muslims journey from around the world to visit their religion's Holy City. Like Malcolm, the great majority of them choose to visit during the Muslim month of Dhu'l-Hijja (roughly overlapping our April) on a special journey called a *hajj.* For Muslim men who are able, it is considered a duty to make the trip at least once during their lifetime. It is also a deeply joyful experience. It gives them a unique opportunity to visit the birthplace of their religion's founder, and to meet fellow believers from all around the world.

For the previous 12 years, Malcolm X had served as a minister of the *Nation of Islam,* an African-American religious movement in the United States. Founded in the early 1930s by Wallace D. Fard, the Nation of Islam was headquartered in Chicago, Illinois, under the leadership of the Honorable Elijah Muhammad. Its members worshiped *Allah,* the god of Muslims throughout the world, and studied the *Koran,* the Holy Book of Islam. But they had little contact with the millions of Muslims in Africa and Asia, and they preached an angry doctrine of racial separation that was unfamiliar to Muslims elsewhere.

Although Elijah Muhammad and other members of the Nation of Islam had journeyed to Mecca in the past, Malcolm X was the first of its members actually to make the hajj. He was overwhelmed by the beauty and the grandeur of the Holy City, and quickly forgot the conflicts and pressures of his life in New York. Together with countless other Muslims, Malcolm took part in the traditional rituals of the hajj. He marched seven times around the Ka'ba, the plain, windowless building that houses the sacred Black Stone in the court of the Great *Mosque*. He bowed and drank water from the Well of Zamzam. He ran seven times back and forth between the Hills al-Safa and al-Marwah. Finally, he climbed with his new friends to the peak of Mount Arafat, the final stage of the hajj.

When the hajj had ended, Malcolm X had become a different person. He had a deeper faith and a whole new way of seeing the world. "I think that the *pilgrimage* to Mecca broadened my [view of humanity] probably more in twelve days than my previous experience during my thirty-nine years on this earth," he told a friend shortly after his arrival back in the United States.

In Malcolm's mind, the most important change concerned the relationship between black people and white people. As a minister of the Nation of Islam, he had preached for years that all white people were devils. Black Americans, he insisted, could only improve their lives by separating themselves as far as possible from the white world.

But now, after eating, sleeping, and worshiping alongside Muslim believers of all colors in Mecca, he was no longer so sure. "The brotherhood! The people of all races, colors, from all over the world coming together as *one!*" he would later explain to an American Muslim. "It has proved to me the power of the One God."

Along with his new attitude, Malcolm had acquired a new, Islamic name, El-Hajj Malik El-Shabazz, and a new look. In place of the stern, clean-shaven appearance of the years before, he now sported a dark, wispy beard. And if the reporters could have seen beneath the tall wool hat he was wearing that spring afternoon at Kennedy International Airport, they would also have noticed that his hair had grown longer. This too was in stark contrast to the close-cropped haircuts worn by men of the Nation of Islam.

*While in Mecca, Malcolm X worshiped alongside
Muslim believers of all races and nationalities.*

Back in the States, things were changing
too. In cities across the country, relations between
blacks and whites had grown very tense during the
five weeks that Malcolm had been away. Many
people were predicting a summer of violence and

rioting. Angry black youths were threatening to take up arms against the police.

In the Harlem district of New York City, there were widespread rumors that a gang calling itself the Blood Brothers was planning to wage war against white shop owners in the *ghetto*. According to some reports, Malcolm X himself was behind the gang, providing gang members with training and support.

Few people actually believed that Malcolm X had played an active role in such a scheme. But in the past, Malcolm had said many angry things to the press in his struggle against white *racism*. Some of these words were spoken to hostile reporters in the heat of the moment, and he later regretted what he had said. Once, when a black man had been murdered in the South, Malcolm had snapped at a group of white reporters, "The Negroes should not wait for white investigators. They should find the guilty ones themselves and kill them on the spot."

And now Malcolm X was back in New York, facing the same hostile reporters with the same accusing questions. "What about the Blood Brothers who are killing innocent white people?" one reporter shouted as soon as Malcolm stepped into the crowd. "Is it true that you are behind them?" Malcolm paused for a second and then answered. He had heard nothing about the gang, he assured the crowd. But he considered all black people to be his "blood brothers."

"What about your suggestion that Negroes should form rifle clubs?" another man called out from the back. "Don't you think this will lead to violence in the streets?" Again Malcolm X was ready. Everyone agreed that it was perfectly acceptable for white people to own guns in order to protect themselves. "It's all right," he said angrily. "It's fine—until *black men* teach it!"

Most of the questions concerned his trip to Mecca. Was it true, the reporters all wanted to know, that Malcolm had experienced a change of heart about white people? Malcolm admitted that he had spoken too broadly in the past. It was wrong to blame all white people for the sins of a few. "I never will be guilty of that again," he assured the reporters. "I know now that some white people *are* truly sincere, that some truly are capable of being brotherly toward a black man."

In Mecca, Malcolm had met many white people who treated him with dignity and respect. But that had only made him more determined to fight for racial justice in the United States. "No matter how much respect, no matter how much recognition whites show towards me," he proclaimed, "as far as I'm concerned, as long as it is not shown to every one of our people in this country, it doesn't exist for me."

A group of Ku Klux Klansmen parade through the streets of a northern city in 1924. The Klan, which preaches a message of white supremacy, was formed in the South at the close of the Civil War. Its campaign of terror and racial hatred played a major role in Malcolm's childhood.

2
Malcolm Little

Malcolm X learned to hate and fear white people at an early age. A few weeks before he was born on May 19, 1925, a gang of angry, hooded Klansmen galloped on horseback to the front door of his parent's home just outside of Omaha, Nebraska. (The Ku Klux Klan is an organization that was formed in the American South shortly after the Civil War. The Klan's members believe that whites are superior to people of other races.) Waving their rifles and shotguns in the air above their heads, the men shouted for Malcolm's father to come out and face them. Trembling at the doorway, Malcolm's mother, Louise Little, informed the Klansmen that she was all alone with her three small children. Her husband, a Baptist minister, was away for the week in Milwaukee, Wisconsin, where he was leading a revival meeting.

But the news only made the men angrier. It was the Reverend Earl Little's preaching, they shouted, that was causing all the trouble in the first place. A follower of Marcus Garvey and his Universal Negro Improvement Association, Malcolm's father had been spreading discontent among black people in Omaha and the surrounding area. From his pulpit, he instructed the members of his congregation to separate themselves from the white community. A day was coming, he predicted, when Garvey would lead them all back to their African homeland.

"Tell him to get out of town," one of the Klansmen yelled as the gang rode away into the night. "We don't want him stirring up any more trouble among the good Negroes of Omaha."

Earl Little was a large, powerful man, standing almost six feet four inches tall. He was not easily frightened. But he had learned to take such threats seriously. As a child in the small town of Reynolds, Georgia, Earl had lost four of his six brothers to violent deaths. One of them had been lynched by a gang of angry Klansmen, much like the one that had threatened Earl's wife and family.

Earl wanted his own family to be safe from the hatred and violence that had tormented his childhood. Shortly after Malcolm was born, the family moved north, first to Milwaukee and then to Lansing, Michigan. There the Reverend Little hoped that he would be able to continue preaching Marcus Garvey's message of racial pride without putting his family in danger.

The Littles soon learned, however, that life for blacks in Michigan was not much different than in Georgia or Nebraska. When Malcolm was four years old, the Klan's nightriders visited again. This time, two white men set fire to the Little's house with torches before Malcolm's father was able to scare them away with his pistol. Malcolm would later describe the scene as the earliest and most vivid memory of his childhood.

"Our home was burning down around us," he told his biographer Alex Haley years later. "We were lunging and bumping and tumbling all over each other trying to escape. My mother, with the baby in her arms, just made it into the yard before the house crashed in, showering sparks. I remember we were outside in the night . . . crying and yelling our heads off."

Once more the family moved, this time to a small farm east of the all-black section of the city. One afternoon Malcolm came home from school to find his parents in the middle of a terrible fight. Louise and Earl Little were both proud, hot-tempered people, and they often argued. But this time they were both angrier than usual. As soon as Malcolm entered the house, his father stormed through the doorway and began walking along the dirt road toward town.

Late that night the police arrived. They took Louise to a hospital to identify the body of her husband. Earl Little had been murdered. His body had been struck by a streetcar and his skull was crushed on one side. Although it was never proven, Malcolm would always believe that his father was killed by the same white people who had burned his home two years earlier.

After Earl Little's death, the family slowly began to come apart. Within a few months, the money from Earl's life insurance policy had all been spent. Louise and her eight children were left to provide for themselves. While their mother worked day and night, the Little children did what they could to help make ends meet. Malcolm and his brothers, Philbert and Reginald, hunted rabbits, muskrats, and bullfrogs to sell to white families in town. "We would lie quiet until unsuspecting bullfrogs appeared," Malcolm later remembered, "and we would spear them, cut off their legs, and sell them for a nickel a pair."

For several months, Louise Little dated a man from Lansing, whom she hoped to marry. After a while, the man ended the relationship, saying he was frightened by the responsibility of raising eight children. Soon after, Louise Little began to grow more and more depressed. Malcolm would later remember this as the most painful time of his life. "We children watched our anchor giving way," he explained. "It was something terrible that you couldn't get your hands on, yet you couldn't get away from. It was a sensing that something bad was going to happen."

Eventually Malcolm's mother had a complete mental breakdown and was committed to the state psychiatric hospital in Kalamazoo, Michigan. She remained there for the next 26 years. It was left to the courts to decide what would happen to Malcolm and the other Little children. Malcolm's brother and sister, Wilfred and Hilda, were old enough to stay by themselves at home. The rest of the children were divided among several families in the area. Malcolm was sent to live with the Gohannas family, with whom he had already been staying during much of his mother's illness.

Since his father's death, Malcolm had been getting into trouble—fighting, stealing, and skipping school whenever he got the chance. One fateful day, the young prankster defiantly entered class without taking off his hat. As punishment, the teacher made him walk in circles around the room.

On one of his many trips around the room, Malcolm noticed that his teacher was writing on the blackboard. Malcolm was angry over being embarrassed in front of his classmates and could not resist the temptation to leave a tack in the teacher's chair while the man's back was turned. "When [my teacher] turned to sit back down," remembered Malcolm, "I was far from the scene of the crime, circling around the rear of the room. Then he hit the tack, and I heard him holler and

At first, young Malcolm thrived at Mason Junior High School. Although one of the few blacks in the school, he was one of the most popular students, and his grades were among the highest in his class. He lost faith in his education, however, when a well-meaning but racist teacher discouraged him from considering a career as a lawyer.

caught a glimpse of him spraddling up as I disappeared through the door."

Malcolm was neither surprised nor upset to hear that he had been expelled from school for his prank. Leaving school would give him more time to spend at home or to wander around town on his own. He was shocked, however, to learn

24

that his reputation as a troublemaker had finally earned him a trip to reform school.

Before he was to be taken to reform school, Malcolm was sent to a detention home in Mason, 12 miles from Lansing. The detention home was run by a friendly white couple, the Swerleins, who liked Malcolm from the start. After a few weeks, they arranged for him to stay on permanently as part of their family, rather than being transferred to reform school.

In the fall, Malcolm was enrolled in the seventh grade at Mason Junior High School. Though he was relieved to have avoided reform school, the first day of classes was still a frightening experience. Except for the children of one black family, Malcolm was the only black student in the entire school.

At first, Malcolm was shocked by how well he got along with his white classmates. He was active in student affairs, playing on the basketball team and joining a number of clubs. At the beginning of the second semester in Mason, he was even elected class president.

It was during this time that Malcolm met his half-sister Ella, his father's daughter by a previous marriage. Ella was a proud, industrious woman who had worked her way up from a life of poverty in Georgia into the polite society of the Roxbury district of Boston, Massachusetts.

"She was the first really proud black woman I had ever seen in my life," he remembered later. "She was plainly proud of her very dark skin. This was unheard of among Negroes in those days."

When Ella invited him to spend the summer with her in Boston, Malcolm jumped at the chance. Climbing aboard the bus to Boston, however, he wondered if he was ready for his first dose of big-city life. "If someone had hung a sign, '*HICK*,' around my neck, I couldn't have looked much more obvious," he recalled.

That summer in Boston changed Malcolm's life. It was the first time he had seen blacks running their own businesses, managing their own affairs, taking pride in themselves. And he would never forget his first experience of the city, especially Roxbury at night: "Neon lights, nightclubs, pool halls, bars, the cars they drove! Restaurants made the streets smell—rich, greasy, down-home black cooking!"

Back home in Mason, Malcolm did his best to fit in. He studied hard and stayed near the top of his class throughout the remainder of the year. But he grew unhappy as the days passed, and became withdrawn from his classmates. After having spent time in the proud black society of Roxbury, he simply could not adjust to life in Mason. Although the Swerleins and his white teachers and fellow students liked Malcolm, he *perceived* that they looked down on him for being black.

The turning point came one day at the end of English class. Inspired by the example of his half-sister Ella and her friends in Roxbury, Malcolm confided to his teacher, Mr. Ostrowski, that he wanted to be a lawyer when he grew up.

"Malcolm, one of life's first needs is for us to be realistic," smiled Mr. Ostrowski, his hands clasped behind his head. "Don't misunderstand me, now. We all here like you, you know that. But you've got to be realistic about being a nigger. A lawyer—that's no realistic goal for a nigger. You need to think about something that you *can* be. . . . Why don't you plan on carpentry?"

Malcolm would never forget his teacher's words, or the anger and frustration that he felt. If there was no room for a black man to succeed in white society, then he would find another society, one that would recognize his talents and encourage his dreams. "It was then that I began to change inside," Malcolm later remembered.

In the weeks that followed, Malcolm wrote to Ella almost daily, telling her how unhappy he was and that he wished he could live with her in Boston. Within a few months, Ella had arranged to assume official custody of her troubled young half-brother.

At the end of the school year, Malcolm was once again boarding a Greyhound bus bound for Boston, Massachusetts. Only this time, he was not coming back. "All praise is due to Allah that I went to Boston when I did," Malcolm later wrote. "If I hadn't, I'd probably still be a brainwashed black Christian."

*Harlem in the 1940s was a thriving center
of black business and culture. "I was mesmerized,"
Malcolm X later described his reaction to his first
glimpse of Harlem: "This world was where I belonged."*

3

Detroit Red

Malcolm was only 16 years old when he arrived in Boston in the summer of 1940. Still upset from his experience in Mason, he informed Ella that he was sick of school. He wanted to drop out, get a job, and support himself. Ella reluctantly agreed with Malcolm's plans. Her only demand was that he wait a few weeks before looking for work. She wanted him "to take [his] time, to walk around, to travel the buses and subways, and get the feel of Boston," before he tied himself down to a full-time job. She would find work for him when the time came.

Ella hoped that Malcolm would spend most of his time in the fashionable section of Roxbury known as the Hill. The Hill was where the most successful black families lived, the people with professional jobs, nice homes, and good manners. But barely 16 years old, Malcolm was much more attracted to the bright lights and colorful characters of Roxbury's lower-class neighborhoods. He loved nights in the city most of all. He would often walk from one end of town to the other, listening in fascination to the music and laughter that poured out of the pool halls, bars, and cheap restaurants that lined the avenues.

It was during one of these walks that Malcolm first met his friend Malcolm "Shorty" Jarvis. Also a native of Lansing, Michigan, Shorty was working in a cheap, smoke-filled pool hall, racking balls for the customers. Malcolm was immediately impressed with the young man's bright clothes, shiny hair, and hip, confident way of talking. For his part, Shorty was delighted to meet someone from his hometown, even someone so wet behind the ears. "Man, this is a swinging town if you dig it," Shorty laughed. "You're my homeboy—I'm going to school you to the happenings."

To Ella's dismay, the two quickly became best friends. Within a few days, Shorty found Malcolm his first job, shining shoes at the Roseland State Ballroom. There Malcolm met some of the great jazz musicians of the day. Duke Ellington, Count Basie, Lionel Hampton, and Lester Young all sat down to chat with Malcolm as he snapped his shoeshine rag across their feet.

Malcolm used his first paycheck from Roseland to buy a zoot suit. With their baggy trousers, tight waists, and bright colors, zoot suits were the outfit worn by all the young men at the Roseland. Years later, Malcolm still fondly remembered his first "zoot," with its "sky-blue pants thirty inches at the knee and angle-narrowed down to twelve inches at the bottom, and a long coat that pinched my waist and flared out below the knees." To complete the picture, Malcolm added a bright blue hat with a feather in the brim and a gold-plated pocket watch on a long, thick-linked chain.

But the biggest change in Malcolm's appearance came a few weeks later, when Shorty persuaded his young friend to "conk" his hair. The conk was a popular hairstyle of the day among many African Americans. Naturally curly hair was straightened or pressed into waves so that it resembled the hairstyles worn by white people.

To conk Malcolm's hair, Shorty mixed two eggs, two medium-sized potatoes, and a bottle of Red Devil lye in a large bowl. Lye is a powerful solution derived from wood ashes that is often used in making soap. It straightens hair when it is applied directly to the head, but it also burns the skin. Shorty explained the possible side effects before he brushed the mixture onto Malcolm's head. "You know it's going to burn when I comb it in," he warned his young friend. "But the longer you can stand it, the straighter the hair."

At first, Malcolm felt only a warm, tingling sensation on his scalp. But then suddenly his head caught fire. He sat there, gritting his teeth, but his eyes were watering and his nose was running uncontrollably before he could scramble to the washbasin to rinse out the lye. "This was my first real big step toward self-degradation," Malcolm would confess years later. "I endured all of that pain, literally burning my flesh to have it look like a white man's hair."

At the time, Malcolm was proud of the way he looked. He rarely missed a chance to show off his new clothes and his new hairdo in public. He especially longed to impress the attractive young women who filled the Roseland Ballroom every dance night. "Once I really got myself warmed and loosened up, I was snatching partners from among the hundreds of . . . girls along the sidelines—almost every one of them could really dance—and I just about went wild! I was whirling girls so fast their skirts were snapping!"

While Malcolm's social life was a great success, his work record was not. Increasingly restless, he often skipped work the way he had cut school back in Mason. He was arrogant and rude to the customers and he was constantly losing jobs.

Ella was desperate to get her younger brother out of Boston and away from Shorty. Finally, she found Malcolm a job working for the railroad, selling sandwiches to passengers aboard the Yankee Clipper, a crowded commuter train that ran each day from Boston to New York. Malcolm was thrilled. His biggest ambition was to see New York City and the thriving black neighborhood of Harlem. In order to qualify for the job, he had to be 21 years old. But the tired old clerk who hired Malcolm "never lifted his eyes from his pencil" when the tall, eager 16-year-old listed his age as 21.

"I was mesmerized," Malcolm later recalled of his first glimpse of Harlem. "This world was where I belonged." Standing on the corner of 125th Street and Lenox Avenue, Malcolm watched in awe. An endless stream of black people lined the sidewalks around him, pouring in and out of the countless shops, restaurants, and music halls that dotted the avenues and side streets of the city. Malcolm was eager to visit all the places that Shorty had told him about. He could hardly wait to see the Apollo Theater and the Savoy Ballroom, where popular artists such as Billie Holiday and Charlie Parker performed almost every night.

But the first place that Malcolm visited was Small's Paradise, one of the hottest night spots in Harlem. Walking into the bar, Malcolm was immediately struck by the conservative manner in which the patrons were dressed and the polite, sophisticated way they behaved toward one another. "Wherever I'd seen as many as ten Boston Negroes . . . drinking," he later explained, "there had been a big noise. But with all of these Harlemites drinking and talking, there was just a low murmur of sound. . . . Their manners seemed natural; they were not putting on any airs."

Despite Ella's disapproval, he moved his things to Harlem, renting a tiny room in a cheap Harlem boardinghouse and taking a job waiting tables at Small's. Malcolm soon became such a regular at the club that the bartender would begin

The first place Malcolm visited in Harlem was Small's Paradise, one of the city's hottest night spots. He soon became such a regular that the bartender began pouring his favorite brand of bourbon as soon as he walked through the door.

pouring his favorite brand of bourbon the second he walked through the door.

Almost everyone at Small's had a nickname. There, Malcolm rubbed shoulders with colorful characters such as Cadillac Drake, West Indian Archie, Dollarbill, and Sammy the Pimp. It was during this period that Malcolm earned his first nickname, "Detroit Red." "Detroit" referred to the largest city near Malcolm's hometown of Lansing, Michigan. He was called "Red" because of his naturally reddish hair and bronze complexion.

Many of the people that Malcolm met at Small's were well-known criminals in Harlem. Their colorful nicknames were used to hide their real identities from the police. Malcolm soon became intrigued by the talk of "easy money" that he heard in Small's. He decided to get some of this easy money for himself. Malcolm's first *"hustle"* was selling marijuana cigarettes to customers at the bar. He also became involved in prostitution, arranging "dates" for the crowds of eager tourists and soldiers who poured into the club each evening.

But Malcolm was young and careless, and it was only a matter of time before he was caught. He was finally arrested one evening after giving a prostitute's phone number to an undercover police officer. Because it was his first offense, Malcolm did not spend any time in jail—but he was permanently barred from Small's.

Malcolm still had plenty of connections in Harlem, however. One of them, his friend Sammy the Pimp, found him work selling marijuana cigarettes on the street. Before long, Malcolm was making more money than he had ever seen before. He also was developing a serious drug habit.

The more successful Malcolm became, the less secure he felt. The police began following him, looking for a chance to arrest him with drugs in his possession. Malcolm knew that if he were arrested a second time he would probably go to prison. And there were rival drug dealers as well, who were jealous of Malcolm's success. Some of his former cronies from Small's even began to treat him with suspicion and contempt. His old friend West Indian Archie put the word out that he was planning to kill Malcolm over an unpaid debt.

Soon Malcolm was carrying a gun and looking over his shoulder wherever he went. He knew that it was only a matter of time before his luck ran out. Finally, after almost four years of living by his wits, the pressure became too much, and Malcolm caught a train back to Boston. "Everything was building up, closing in on me," he later explained. "Up to that point, I'd been lucky enough, or slick enough, to escape jail . . . or any *serious* trouble. But I knew that any minute now something had to give."

In spite of all the money that he had made in New York, Malcolm was completely broke when he arrived in Boston. He had lost a lot of the money gambling, but most of it went to support his worsening drug habit. He spent more than $20 a day for cocaine, while another $5 were spent on marijuana and cigarettes.

Desperate, he persuaded his white girlfriend, Sophia, and her sister, along with his old friend Shorty, to join him in robbing wealthy homes in Boston. Malcolm's plan was simple. The women would explore the fashionable white neighborhoods of Boston during the day, looking for houses whose wealthy owners were away.

Then Malcolm and Shorty would perform the robbery at night, with the women driving the getaway car.

The burglary spree lasted for almost a year, finally ending when Malcolm was arrested in a jewelry store in Boston. Malcolm had taken a stolen watch to a repair shop to replace a broken crystal. The police were waiting when Malcolm returned a couple of days later to pick up the watch. They arrested him before he was able to reach for the gun he kept in the holster beneath his coat. Otherwise, he would almost certainly have been killed.

The police found everything in Malcolm's apartment: the stolen goods, the burglary equipment, and Malcolm's small arsenal of guns. With the state's overwhelming evidence, Malcolm was not surprised to hear the verdict of the jury or the judge's harsh decision. Along with Shorty, he was found guilty on 14 counts of burglary and sentenced to 10 years in the Charlestown State Prison.

Suddenly, Malcolm found himself confined to a tiny prison cell. Deprived of the drugs that he had been taking every day for years, he was "physically miserable and as evil-tempered as a snake." At first, he was so out of control that he was nicknamed "Satan" by his fellow inmates.

Malcolm was the first one to admit that being sent to prison was the great turning point in his life. It was in prison, after all, that he was transformed from an angry, desperate, almost suicidal young man into a confident, articulate Muslim disciple. But he would never forget, nor forgive, the suffering and indignity that he experienced living behind bars. "Any person who claims to have deep feeling for other human beings," he would later insist, "should think a long, long time before he votes to have other men kept behind bars—caged. I am not saying that there shouldn't be prisons, but there shouldn't be bars. Behind bars, a man never reforms. He will never forget. He never will get completely over the memory of the bars."

In Charlestown State Prison, Malcolm slowly began to transform himself from a desperate, young street hustler into a confident, articulate Muslim disciple.

CHAPTER

4

Malcolm X

In prison, Malcolm slowly began to reform himself. Away from the drugs, the alcohol, and the pressure of the streets, he could finally see what a mess his life had become during the previous four years in Roxbury and Harlem. It terrified him to realize how close he had come to death on a number of occasions, and how he had often deliberately put himself in danger.

"Looking back, I think I really was at least slightly out of my mind," he later confessed. "I viewed narcotics as most people regard food. I wore my guns as today I wear my neckties. Deep down, I actually believed that after living as fully as humanly possible, one should then die violently. I think I deliberately invited death in many, sometimes insane ways."

The first person to have a real impact on Malcolm's life in prison was a fellow inmate named Bimbi. A tall, quiet, fair-skinned black man, Bimbi was one of the prison's old-timers. During the day, Bimbi worked alongside Malcolm making automobile license plates, but he spent his evenings in the prison library, reading books on history, religion, and political science.

Malcolm was immediately impressed by the way the older prisoner could talk freely on a number of topics, and by the large groups that would crowd around Bimbi whenever he began to speak—including the white prison guards. "What fascinated me with him most of all," Malcolm later explained, "was that he was the first man I had ever seen command total respect . . . with his words."

Malcolm had only completed the eighth grade before leaving Mason, and his reading and writing skills were poor. "I didn't know a verb from a house," he later joked. But with Bimbi's patient assistance, Malcolm gradually began to improve. Before long, he was writing long letters to his family and joining Bimbi in the prison library at night. Once Malcolm began reading, nothing could stop him. After the lights were turned off each night at 10 o'clock, he would often read for hours by the faint glow of the lamp at the other end of the hallway.

During this time, Malcolm learned that his brother Philbert had joined a religious community called the Nation of Islam. "Pray to Allah for deliverance," Philbert wrote to his younger brother. The letter was signed by Philbert, but it seemed to Malcolm that it could have been written by someone else because of its unfamiliar phrases and polite, formal tone; these were a result of his brother's conversion.

A few weeks later, an even stranger letter arrived from Malcolm's brother Reginald. "Malcolm," the letter insisted, "don't eat any more pork, and don't smoke any more cigarettes. I'll show you how to get out of prison." In his cell that evening, Malcolm read the letter again and again. He had no idea what Reginald had in mind. But if it could help him get out of prison, then he was certainly willing to give it a chance.

When Reginald finally visited Malcolm a few weeks later, he admitted that he did not really have a plan to get him out of prison. He had told Malcolm that, and not to eat pork or smoke, in order to get his attention. Reginald insisted, however, that what he was offering Malcolm was something much more important. He claimed that he had discovered the true religion, a religion that would finally deliver blacks from their years of suffering in white society.

As the two men talked in the prison waiting room, Reginald began to explain to Malcolm all that he had learned about his new faith. Though much that he heard seemed strange and un-familiar, Malcolm was able to follow the basic story. "God had come to America," Reginald claimed, and had revealed himself to a man named the Honorable Elijah Muhammad. A slight, gentle man, Elijah Muhammad had moved his family from Macon, Georgia, to Detroit, Michigan, in 1923. There he had met a mysterious man named Master Wallace D. Fard, whom he claimed was "God in person." From Master Fard, Elijah Muhammad learned the "true knowledge" of the religion of Islam.

Master Fard taught Elijah Muhammad that the first people on earth were black. They had a great civilization, far more advanced than any-thing we have today. For years, these first people lived together in peace, worshiping Allah in the Holy City of Mecca. One day, a mad scientist named Yacub used his knowledge to invent an evil race of white devils. It was these devils who en-slaved the black race, taking them away from their homes and robbing them of their language and

Elijah Muhammad, the quiet-spoken but all-powerful head of the Nation of Islam, immediately recognized Malcolm's potential as a minister for the Muslim religion. From prison, Malcolm wrote letters almost daily to the Muslim leader.

their identity. Master Fard claimed that he himself was the black messiah, sent by Allah to lead black people to a heavenly paradise here on earth.

Malcolm's life was immediately changed. He wrote Elijah Muhammad at his home in Chicago. He told the Muslim leader how the news of

Islam had reached him in prison. Malcolm was also full of questions about the Muslim religion, questions that he felt only the Honorable Elijah Muhammad could answer. The more Malcolm learned about his new faith, the more questions he had. Soon he was writing to Elijah Muhammad almost every day.

Elijah Muhammad was not the only person to whom Malcolm wrote during his final days in prison. He sent letters to his old friends in Roxbury and Harlem, telling them about his new life as a follower of Islam. He wrote to the mayor of Boston and the governor of Massachusetts, telling them that they were responsible for the horrible conditions under which black people suffered in white society. He even wrote an angry letter to Harry S Truman, the president of the United States.

In addition to writing, Malcolm also continued to read. If anything, he had become even more passionate in his love for books. But now his reading had a purpose. Malcolm wanted to spread the word of Elijah Muhammad to his fellow inmates. In order to persuade others to accept the message of Islam, Malcolm reasoned, he would have to prepare himself to respond to all of their questions. The more he learned, the more prepared he would be.

Malcolm's studies paid off. He became an effective preacher. By his words and his example, he led many of his fellow black inmates to follow the Muslim religion. He quickly discovered what Elijah Muhammad already knew. Black prisoners were often the easiest converts to the Nation of Islam's message of black pride and racial separation.

"Usually the convict comes from among those bottom-of-the-pile Negroes," Malcolm later explained, "the Negroes who through their entire lives have been kicked about, treated like children—Negroes who have never met one white man who didn't either take something from them or do something to them. . . . That's why black prisoners become Muslims so fast when Elijah

Muhammad's teachings filter into their cages by way of other Muslim convicts. 'The white man is the devil' is a perfect echo of that black convict's lifelong experience."

When Malcolm was finally released from prison in August 1952, he went to live at the home of his brother Wilfred. Also a recent convert to Islam, Wilfred owned a furniture store in Detroit. When Malcolm was not at work in his brother's store, he could often be found attending meetings at Detroit's Temple Number One. Malcolm was thrilled to discover that Detroit's Temple was the first to be formed by the Nation of Islam and was actually founded by Master Fard in 1931.

Malcolm was immediately impressed by the tasteful dress of his brothers and sisters at Temple Number One and the mature, confident way in which they carried themselves. He was distressed from the beginning, however, by how few people actually attended the Wednesday, Friday, and Sunday evening meetings held each week. If the Honorable Elijah Muhammad and his followers were really preaching the truth for the black race, Malcolm insisted, then blacks should be beating down the doors to hear what they had to say. They should be standing in line, the way they had waited patiently to see Billie Holiday or Duke Ellington at the Apollo Theater in Harlem. "I thought it was outrageous that our small temple still had some empty seats," he later said.

Before long, Malcolm was putting his outrage to good use, recruiting followers around the neighborhood. Elijah Muhammad had recently encouraged Malcolm to seek out the young people in the community, and he had set up a special ministry just for them. In addition, Malcolm had begun to take the Nation of Islam's message to the barrooms and pool halls of black Detroit, where the poorest and most destitute black people often congregated. Malcolm was constantly frustrated by how few people responded to his message. But gradually the pews of Temple Number One began to fill, and people began to talk about the exciting young minister in the community.

It was during this time that Malcolm received his X. Elijah Muhammad taught his followers that white Americans had robbed black people of their true African names. The X stood for this true family name that had been lost when Africans had been taken into slavery. But for Malcolm, the name meant even more. It represented all the bad habits and self-defeating attitudes that he had now left behind. "Ex-smoker. Ex-drinker. Ex-Christian. Ex-slave," he said proudly of his new identity.

Not surprisingly, Elijah Muhammad himself began to take a personal interest in Malcolm's work at Temple Number One. Gradually, he began to send his young disciple to other cities to win new followers the way he had done in Detroit. In little more than a year, Malcolm became the most highly regarded young minister in the entire Nation of Islam. Finally, in June of 1954, Malcolm was sent to tiny Temple Number Seven in New York. After almost 10 years, he was going back to Harlem.

In Harlem, Malcolm sought out many of his old friends. He was saddened to learn that Sammy the Pimp had died, but he visited Cadillac Drake and West Indian Archie soon after his arrival. Many of Malcolm's old friends were mistrustful of his newfound faith. Remembering Malcolm from the old days, they doubted that he had become a minister of Islam and wondered what he was really doing. But if Malcolm's old friends were not open to his message, there were plenty of people who were. Temple Number Seven slowly began to grow into one of the busiest and most respected Muslim congregations in the country.

In 1958, Malcolm married Sister Betty Sanders, a young woman from Temple Number Seven in Harlem. In the past, Malcolm had said many disturbing things about women. He had accused them of trying to rob men of their dignity and self-respect. Because of Sister Betty, however, Malcolm began to change many of his views. Though the couple had many disagreements, their relationship was filled with love and respect. Slowly,

Malcolm began to view women as partners, and not enemies, in the struggle for racial justice.

Although Malcolm would soon become a world figure, meeting with presidents and heads of state, he was still at his best on the streets

By the mid-1950s, Malcolm X had become the most respected young minister in the Nation of Islam. Though he was appointed full-time minister of Temple Number Seven in Harlem in 1954, he often traveled across the country to recruit new members for the movement.

of Harlem. "It was always a strange and moving experience to walk with Malcolm in Harlem," wrote M. S. Handler in 1965. "He was known to all. People glanced at him shyly. Sometimes youngsters would ask for his autograph. . . . They looked upon Malcolm with a certain wonderment. Here was a man who had come from the lower depths which they still inhabited, who had triumphed over his own criminality and his own ignorance to become a forceful leader and spokesman, an uncompromising champion of his people."

For years, Malcolm did everything in his power to deflect all of this attention. He wanted everyone to know that it was the Honorable Elijah Muhammad, not Malcolm X, who preached the real message of deliverance for black people in America. Malcolm insisted again and again that he was only Muhammad's disciple. But increasingly, it was Malcolm, not Elijah Muhammad, who gained the attention of the white media and the affection of many Muslim believers. Malcolm feared correctly that this would eventually cause conflicts in the Nation of Islam, and a rift between himself and Elijah Muhammad.

Problems began in 1959, when CBS Television aired a documentary called *The Hate That Hate Produced*. The program gave white America its first glimpse of the Nation of Islam, and presented Malcolm X as a handsome, angry young champion of racial justice. A number of magazine articles and television interviews followed, each giving Malcolm more public exposure. In 1962, author Alex Haley—who had previously interviewed Malcolm—informed Elijah Muhammad that Grove Press was interested in publishing an autobiography of Malcolm X, written by Haley and Malcolm. Elijah Muhammad agreed, realizing that the book would bring the Nation of Islam more converts. There were others within the Nation of Islam, however, who were not as comfortable with Malcolm's growing popularity. They began to spread rumors that Malcolm was hungry for power. His real goal, they claimed, was to replace Elijah Muhammad as the leader of the

Nation of Islam. Little by little, Elijah Muhammad began to lose faith in Malcolm X.

The final break came in November 1963, following the *assassination* of President John F. Kennedy. Fearing anger from the white community, Elijah Muhammad had instructed his ministers to refuse to comment to the press about the incident. In the heat of an interview, Malcolm ignored the order. He told a reporter that Kennedy's death was a case of "the chickens coming home to roost." Malcolm meant that white Americans had allowed hatred and *bigotry* to continue for too long. In the past, only black people, like Malcolm's father, had been killed. Now, no one was safe from hatred and violence, not even the president.

The next day, Malcolm's quote was in the headlines of all the papers. Elijah Muhammad was furious, and suspended Malcolm from his position as National Minister and his work at Temple Number Seven. After a few weeks, Malcolm began to realize that Elijah Muhammad had no intention of restoring him to his position as minister. After 12 years of faithful service, Malcolm was being quietly forced out of the Nation of Islam.

As things began to fall apart around him, Malcolm began to look inward. He spent more and more time reading the Koran, the Holy Book of Islam. If his own community had rejected him, he reasoned, then he would seek fellowship among the remaining 750 million Muslims throughout the world. He made plans to build a Moslem mosque in Harlem to compete with Temple Number Seven. He also gathered information about making a journey to Mecca, Islam's Holy City. Every Muslim man is required to travel to Mecca at least once during his lifetime, if he is able. Malcolm believed that his time had finally come.

When Malcolm X returned from Mecca in the spring of
1964, he sported a longer, fuller haircut and a dark,
wispy beard. He also had a new Muslim name, El-Hajj
Malik El-Shabazz.

5
The
Final Days

The trip to Mecca was the greatest thrill of Malcolm X's life. There he discovered that true Islam was not a doctrine of hatred and separation. Allah is the one God, teaches the Koran. And it is Allah's will that all people live together as one, regardless of race or color. "Never have I witnessed," he wrote during his trip to Mecca, "such sincere hospitality and the overwhelming spirit of true brotherhood as is practiced by people of all colors and races here in this Ancient Holy Land."

Malcolm had seen firsthand that blacks and whites could live together in harmony. He had eaten and slept and worshiped alongside Muslim believers of all races. "Perhaps," he wrote to a friend in the United States, "if white Americans could accept the Oneness of God, then perhaps, too, they could accept *in reality* the Oneness of Man—and cease to measure, and hinder, and harm others in terms of their 'differences' in color."

Until that happened, however, Malcolm felt that he had no choice but to continue his fight for racial justice back home. One way that Malcolm hoped to do this was by forming a movement that would unite the struggles of black people in Africa and the United States. "Can you imagine what can happen," he told one reporter, "what would certainly happen, if all [black] people ever *realize* their blood bonds, if they ever realize they have a common goal—if they ever *unite?*"

To help achieve this, Malcolm had formed the Organization of Afro-American Unity the previous year. The name was inspired by a group that was already bringing together black people across Africa, called the Organization of African Unity. To gain support for his new project, Malcolm traveled to meet with many important black leaders in Africa, including Kwame Nkrumah, the founder of modern Ghana, and Prime Minister Jomo Kenyatta of Kenya.

Malcolm returned home to one of the most violent summers in American history. Across the United States, blacks were beginning to express their anger and frustration over centuries of poverty and racial *oppression*. There were angry *protests* and race riots in cities around the country.

While many people in the black community looked to Malcolm for guidance and leadership, others regarded him with suspicion. To some, Malcolm's angry words had fueled the fires that were now burning in many American cities. For others, Malcolm had not done enough to support the struggle. Black leaders such as Martin Luther King, Jr., and James Farmer had been active in protests and marches, often risking imprisonment or injury. But Malcolm, many insisted, had stayed safely behind his pulpit or podium. He spoke angry, defiant words, but he rarely did anything to put his ideas into practice.

Malcolm X's marriage to Sister Betty Sanders in 1958 was one of the most important events in his life. Pictured here with one of his daughters, Malcolm X became increasingly devoted to his family toward the end of his life, and more open to the contributions of women in the struggle for racial justice.

Malcolm's greatest problems came from the Nation of Islam. Not only had the community turned its back on him, but troubling rumors had now begun to circulate. In Harlem, the word on the street was that someone in the Nation of Islam wanted to kill Malcolm.

Throughout the remainder of the year, Malcolm met frequently with reporters, *civil rights* activists, and community leaders, trying to generate support for his Organization of Afro-American Unity. He continued to hold regular meetings with his followers, still hoping to build a Muslim mosque in Harlem. He met every chance he could with author Alex Haley. The two men had almost finished Malcolm's autobiography. They had been working together on the book for more than two years.

Then, in the beginning of 1965, things began to come apart. Early one morning, someone tossed a firebomb through the living room window of Malcolm's home. Fire fighters arrived in time to save most of the family's possessions, but the house was almost completely destroyed. As he stumbled out of the house, his arms full of clothing and books, Malcolm's heart sank at the sight in front of him. Betty and the children stood helpless in the middle of the yard, coughing and crying and still in their pajamas. It was an eerie reminder of the violence that had disrupted his own childhood in Michigan.

Representatives of the Nation of Islam told reporters that their organization had nothing to do with the fire. They claimed that Malcolm had started the blaze himself to generate publicity for the new movement he was forming. But Malcolm knew that it was only a matter of time before he would be attacked again.

In the days that followed, Malcolm tried his best to stay busy. But he could never forget that there were people following him, just waiting for an opportunity to kill him. "He kept looking over his shoulder," remembered one of his friends. "It was spooky." In one of the last interviews for his autobiography, Malcolm told Alex

Haley that he did not expect to live long enough to see the finished book. As the days passed, the tension became even greater. Once, when a friend called Malcolm about an appointment the following Tuesday, Malcolm stated flatly, "I'll be dead by Tuesday."

If he had to die now, Malcolm hoped that at least his death would help people to see the real costs of violence and hatred. "I know that societies often have killed the people who have helped to change those societies," he wrote shortly before his death. "And if I can die having brought any light, having exposed any meaningful truth that will help to destroy the racist cancer that is malignant in the body of America—then, all of the credit is due to Allah."

The end finally came on the afternoon of February 21, 1965. Malcolm was scheduled to address a group of followers at the Audubon Ballroom in Harlem. Malcolm smiled as he walked to the podium to greet the small group that had come to hear him speak. Suddenly, in the middle of the crowd a disturbance broke out; two men were shouting at each other. Malcolm raised his hand to calm them. "Hold it! Hold it! Don't get excited," Malcolm said. Suddenly, three men in the front row rose to their feet, firing guns toward the podium. A spray of bullets hit Malcolm's body, including one shotgun blast in the center of his chest. He fell backward to the floor, crashing into the two chairs behind him. He was probably dead before he hit the ground.

The Autobiography of Malcolm X was published in November of 1965. Already, the arguments over Malcolm's legacy had begun. In churches, in prisons, on the streets of inner cities across America, people were asking the same questions. Who was Malcolm X? What were his real beliefs about violence and armed resistance? Did he really think that blacks and whites could ever live together peacefully? What would he have done if he had not been assassinated?

Today, Malcolm has once again captured the imagination of the public. Across America,

Malcolm X returns home on the morning of February 14, 1965, to inspect the damage caused to his house by a firebomb. The Nation of Islam claimed that he had started the fire himself to gain publicity.

thousands of young people wear X's on their hats and pictures of Malcolm X on their T-shirts. In 1992, film director Spike Lee's movie, *Malcolm X*, offered a moving portrayal of Malcolm by actor Denzel Washington. And after almost 30 years, *The Autobiography of Malcolm X* is back on the best-seller list.

For many people, the questions about Malcolm remain. What would he have been like if he had lived? And who in the African-American community is best qualified to speak on his behalf? Sadly, these are questions that we will never be able to answer. Chances are, however, that, had Malcolm lived, *he* would be the one asking the questions. Malcolm was never afraid to ask the most difficult questions, either of himself or of other people. Sometimes the answers he found were not the ones that he expected, or the ones that he desired. But he was always open to the difficult lessons that life taught him. And he was always willing to change his life and his beliefs to reflect what he had learned. Perhaps it was this tireless commitment to justice and truth, whatever the costs, that continues to captivate us and to disturb us.

"Despite my firm convictions," Malcolm X wrote shortly before his death, "I have always been a man who tries to face facts, and to accept the reality of life as new experience and new knowledge unfolds it. I have always kept an open mind, which is necessary to the flexibility that must go hand in hand with every form of intelligent search for truth."

Further Reading

Davis, Thulani. *Malcolm X: The Great Photographs.* New York: Stewart, Tabori & Chang, 1993.

Goldman, Peter. *The Death and Life of Malcolm X.* New York: Harper and Row, 1973.

Halasa, Malu. *Elijah Muhammad: Religious Leader.* New York: Chelsea House, 1990.

Malcolm X. *By Any Means Necessary.* Edited by George Breitman. New York: Pathfinder Press, 1967.

———. *Malcolm X Talks to Young People.* New York: Pathfinder Press, 1965.

Malcolm X and Alex Haley. *The Autobiography of Malcolm X.* New York: Grove Press, 1965.

Myers, Walter Dean. *Malcolm X: By Any Means Necessary.* New York: Scholastic, 1993.

Rummel, Jack. *Malcolm X: Militant Black Leader.* New York: Chelsea House, 1989.

Glossary

Allah   the Supreme Being of the Islamic religion

assassination   murder, especially of a politically important person

bigotry   the idea that one's own opinions and judgments are superior to those of others

civil rights   the personal and property rights recognized by a government and guaranteed by its laws and constitution

ghetto   a section of a city occupied by members of a single minority group

hajj   a special trip to the city of Mecca made by a Muslim man at least once in his life if possible

hick   an unkind name for an unsophisticated or simple person

hustle   making money by cheating or in an unlawful manner

Islam   a religion based on the teachings of the prophet Muhammad and on the worship of Allah

74

Koran   the Holy Book of Islam written by the religion's founder, Muhammad

Mecca   the Holy City of Islam in Saudi Arabia

mosque   a Muslim house of worship

Muslim   a follower of the Islamic religion

Nation of Islam   an African-American religious movement connected to Islam

oppression   the unjust or cruel exercise of power or authority over others

perceive   to become aware of

pilgrimage   a journey to a sacred place

protest   a public expression of disapproval

racism   a belief that one's own race is superior

Chronology

1925   Malcolm X is born under the name Malcolm Little in Omaha, Nebraska, on May 19.

1931   Malcolm's father is murdered.

1942   Malcolm becomes a street hustler in New York City.

1946   He is sentenced to 10 years in prison for robbery.

1948   Malcolm begins to write to Elijah Muhammad; he converts to the Nation of Islam and changes his name to Malcolm X.

1952   He is paroled from prison.

1953   Malcolm X is appointed a minister for the Nation of Islam; he organizes his first temple in Boston, Massachusetts.

1954   Malcolm X is appointed minister of the Nation of Islam's temple in New York City.

1958 He marries Sister Betty Sanders.

1962 Malcolm X is appointed national minister of the Nation of Islam.

1964 Malcolm X leaves the Nation of Islam; he makes a religious pilgrimage to the Middle East and changes his name to El-Hajj Malik El-Shabazz; he goes on a speaking tour of Africa, during which he founds the Organization of Afro-American Unity.

1965 Malcolm X is assassinated in New York City on February 21.

Index

Autobiography of Malcolm X, The (Haley), 59, 67, 68, 70, 71

Bimbi, 46, 47
Boston, Massachusetts, 29, 31, 36, 41, 42

Detroit, Michigan, 49, 54, 55

Fard, Wallace D., 9, 49, 50, 53

Haley, Alex, 20, 59, 67, 68, 69
Harlem, New York, 13, 36, 37, 39, 40, 45, 51, 54, 55, 56, 58, 61, 67, 69
Hate That Hate Produced, The (documentary), 59

Islam, 8, 9, 49, 51, 52, 53, 56, 63
Jarvis, Malcolm "Shorty," 32, 33, 34, 36, 41, 42

King, Martin Luther, Jr., 65

Little, Earl (father), 18, 19, 20, 21
  murder, 21
Little, Ella (half-sister), 26, 28, 29, 31, 33, 36, 37
Little, Hilda (sister), 22
Little, Louise (mother), 18, 19, 20, 21, 22
Little, Malcolm. *See* Malcolm X
Little, Philbert (brother), 21, 47
Little, Reginald (brother), 21, 48, 49
Little, Wilfred (brother), 22, 53

Malcolm X
  adolescence, 26–41
  assassination, 69–70
  autobiography, 59, 67, 68, 70, 71
  birth, 19

childhood, 17–29, 68
conflicts with the Nation
  of Islam, 58, 59–61
conversion to Islam, 43,
  47–51, 53
criminal life, 39–42, 58
drug habit, 40, 41, 42,
  43, 45
education, 23–24, 26,
  27, 28, 31
legacy, 70–72
life in Boston, 27, 31,
  35, 41–43
love of reading, 47, 51
marriage to Betty
  Sanders, 56
as minister of Islam, 52,
  54–61
movie, 71
name change, 55
pilgrimage to Mecca, 7–
  15, 61, 63–64
prison experience, 43,
  45–53
release from prison, 53
views on women, 56–57

Malcolm X (movie), 71
Mecca, Saudi Arabia, 8, 10,
  11, 14, 15, 49, 61, 63
Muhammad, Elijah, 9, 49,
  50, 51, 52, 53, 54, 55,
  58, 59, 60
Muslims, 8, 9, 10, 11, 50,
  51, 52, 53, 56, 58, 61,
  67

Nation of Islam, 9, 10, 11,
  47, 52, 53, 54, 55, 59,
  60, 61, 67, 68

Omaha, Nebraska, 17, 18
Organization of Afro-
  American Unity, 64, 67

Roxbury, Massachusetts,
  26, 27, 28, 32, 45, 51

Sanders, Betty (wife), 56,
  66, 68

Temple Number Seven, 55,
  56, 60

David Shirley is a writer and editor living in Brooklyn, New York. In addition to writing the books *Satchel Paige* and *Alex Haley* in Chelsea House's BLACK AMERICANS OF ACHIEVEMENT series, he is the author of *A Good Death* and a contributing editor to *Option* magazine.

Picture Credits